In loving memory of my father, Joseph R. Mangold, Sr., and his loving pal, Sneakers

POETRY HIGHWAY

NO ENTRY

POETRY HIGHWAY

Cheryl "Ashley" Dennin

VANTAGE PRESS
New York

Sponsored by Rich D. Enterprises, Inc.

Published by Vantage Press, Inc.
516 West 34th Street, New York, New York 10001

Manufactured in the United States of America
ISBN: 0-533-12923-0

0 9 8 7 6 5 4 3 2 1

Contents

About the Author

Cheryl "Ashley" Dennin lives in Philadelphia, where she was born and raised. She graduated from Northeast Preparatory School in 1977.

For a brief time in her early twenties, the author attended John Casablanca's school for modeling. After overcoming many obstacles throughout her life, she would like to share the many inspirations of her life through her poetry.

Now that her children are almost grown, Ms. Dennin has more time to do something for herself. Her many inspirations come from life's journeys, love twists, and special individuals, along with moments that have left a mark upon her life.

The author is also a member of the International Society of Poets. She also enjoys music and the company of her friends and family.

POETRY HIGHWAY

The Road of Life

As I follow the path that I go, I'm
thankful to all who encouraged me to do so.
Never say never, it's all in your mind.
Keep thinking positive about everything
and you will do just fine.
Give it your all, never give up.
Making something from nothing makes
the best kinds of stuff!

A Father's Inspiration

Passing to heaven, have you found your way?
Has your spirit forgotten about passing this way?
You never returned to let me know that you arrived
    there okay.
I guess there's no way of knowing;
All you can do is count on what you believe,
that you are with your family, God, and there's no
    place for me.
How you said that "I love you" stuff and laughed at
    the Morts' lies.
Can't you sense from heaven I'm calling your spirit
    to my eyes?
For I know I'm being selfish for wanting not to let
    go.
You were the greatest person; heaven's where you
    are I know.
Maybe in time you'll find your way back and let me
    know that heaven's where it's at!
Now that you're gone, you know how much you
    really meant.
I'll go on believing that it was a blessed time spent.

My Daughter and I

A daughter is unique in many different ways.
She's someone who can relate to you in a very
    special way.
A daughter needs a special love, only a mother can
    give.
She needs you to be her friend, as well!
She needs confidence from within.
She knows she can always count on me and
    together we will win!
Never having any problems speaking about many
    different things.
We always stick together, that's because we're both
    one of a kind.
She knows in her heart I'll always be there for her
    each and every time.

Cheating Hearts

Lost in love, what is there to do?
In love with more than one is totally taboo.
Need help deciding which one to choose?
How can you expect sincerity if someone doubts
     you?
Secrets and lies are the tools that they need.
Justifying to yourself the right to proceed.
Thinking you can have two or more is such a foolish
     dream.
Love isn't for real, it's a big-time scheme.
It's all part of the ego of a lonely man's self-esteem.
There's no exceptions to the rule, a cheating heart's
     nothing but cruel.
Expect the worst, never the best.
You know a cheating heart can never rest.

Wind Storm

As I was awakened by hail-like golf balls,
I moseyed to the window, saying to myself,
"Oh, what a storm!"
I watched as the twister passed before my eyes.
I ran into the closet, thinking this, the first place to
    hide.
I prayed on my hands and knees that it just wasn't
    my time.
Being in the closet was the most difficult part of
    this time.
It happened so quickly, it came and away it went.
When I opened up the door, I didn't know what to
    expect.
Peeking out slowly, I thanked the Lord that
    nothing was damaged by the terrible wind
    storm!

Wanting to Be Like You

Hey over there, you boy named Pierre, do you want
to come out and play some hockey or some
basketball today?

There's only one problem with this, you and your
friends taunt and tantalize me and you just
won't ever quit.

When you or your friends pick on me, hit me, or
make me mad, then I'm being quoted as being
bad!

But it's okay for you, to lie along with your friends
and tease me, hit me, and treat me as you do.

Is my being a little bit different than you, the
reason you also make fun of me too.

The other kids call me strange, but that's not my
name.

All that I want to do is have friends and play the
same way that other children do.

Mental Aches

When I was much younger, I didn't realize what I
    had done.
I got married, following that, I bore a baby son.
As I got older and wiser and realized the true facts,
One of those was knowing that I had grown up
    much too fast.
How can I be at fault now, for sometimes losing my
    cool?
I just don't want to make bad choices, and be just
    anyone else's fool.
My heart sometimes aches for the mistakes and
    other things I'm just too ashamed to admit.
I wish I was someone else at times, but the shoe
    just doesn't fit.
Never knowing then, the consequences that would
    come to exist.
Knowing now that somehow, I'd surely have to
    make that shoe fit!

Forbidden Passion Pleasures

Feelings of the heart and soul have no sin.
The forbidden fruits of passion have secret desires
    from within.
A taste of forbidden passion, there's just no other
    way to face life's scary attractions.
Begging and pleading to change your way of
    existence completely.
Realizing all that you are, is the bleeding rose, with
    thorns of flowing tears, alongside those
    brokenhearted dreams.
Feelings so genuine, unique, and honestly true.
That's human nature, a natural attraction, so what
    do you do?
These are the forbidden passion pleasures, of only
    two!
Women of beauty, so full of life, love and joy.
Though many hearts are broken, and tossed
    around, like tiny wind-up toys.
External beauty doesn't mean, you've got it made,
    and everything is ravishing, traveling along,
    life's mystery highway.
Sadly mistaken, the trustmaker, you see.
Misery looks your way once more, it's factual
    indeed!
Either or, young and carefree or older and wiser,
    somehow your heart still bleeds.
Beyond the rose of sweet red wine, a fine-tasting
    blend that just totally consumes your mind.

Like the rose that cries tears, for pleasures of lovers
in love, trying to fulfill yesterdays stolen,
forgotten, lost dreams.

Superstitious Minds

Seven years break a mirror and see; superstition of
    all sorts
Says that bad luck will follow your shadow, that's
    what will proceed.
The events to follow your shadow might play with
    your mind.
Even make you leery and scary at times.
I bet by now superstition's preying on your mind.
I know you wish, that you could turn back the
    hands of time!
When life was so easy and full of things so divine.
Hoping now that superstition won't constantly
    haunt your inner mind.

A Mother and Her Son

First he's a newborn crying up a storm, pacifying
  this child all day and night long.
I never realized your lungs were so strong.
When you spoke your first words, I was the only
  voice you heard.
As you took your first steps, how I thought I was so
  blessed.
Although you were such a pleasure when you were
  small.
You took every bit of time and energy making sure
  you had it all.
As your son starts to grow, cherish the times
  together 'til he wants to do things all on his
  own.
Always did I make my son my primary concern.
Going on vacations, playing games with your
  friends.
Oh, my son, what a good time you had!
Even having the pleasure of visiting Disneyland.
As much as you might want to, you can never deny
  who you are and who gave you life.
Never did I ask anyone for help.
I always raised you, my son, all by myself!
Did you forget Mommy did her very, very best?
Mommy loves you, so, just don't ever forget this!

Springtime Is Here

Spring is here.
Trees and flowers are blooming this time of year.
Days are longer so that the plants can grow
    stronger.
After they sprout, beautiful blossoms come out.
Bees will be coming, looking for honey.
This is nature's way of bringing out the season full
    of bright sunny days.

Missing Pieces

My life, a mystery of accomplishment I wait.
Serenity is the word I solely "proclamate."
To live and let live, to die and to learn to let go.
People, places, and things follow my footsteps
 wherever I may go.
My mind wanders so very fast, living life present,
 future, and looking back on events of the past.
Days are in a maze; which is the right road I must
 take?
Accomplishment is what I await, as long as it may
 take.
Happiness, which is fine, but where can I find my
 own peace of mind?
What are the many wonders, which my life so
 encumbers?
Help me to find the way to accomplish this journey
 I must take.

Who Am I?

When I was a young boy, I sat around and played
    with my toys.
As I became a little bigger, I would always see, a
    strange woman's image,
Staring at me through my curtain-covered window.
I always would go on and ask, why does this
    woman's image keep coming back?
She just wants to see her little son, growing up,
    seeing him happy, and other types of fun.
After a while, she stopped coming back. I guess I
    was too young then, and didn't understand the
    true facts.
This woman's image, that watched me through my
    curtain-covered glass window,
Was no longer of this earth; she passed away not
    too long after my birth.
I'll never forget her beautiful face, may her soul
    rest alongside, of the mother who took her
    place.
She always did everything for me, and she did it all
    so well indeed.
Many times taking care of me, in sickness and in
    health.
May your souls rest together, forever, the mother
    who raised me and the mother who made me.

Under the Rainbow

Under the rainbow is where we stand.
Two hearts together bonded by a woman and a
    man.
Colors so beautiful, full of purple, red, green,
    yellow, and blue.
Colors of the rainbow are the hearts of me and you.
People together, hearts of all ages intertwine.
Hearts full of love like the rainbow.
Things so beautiful together, so divine.
It's something so special, lasting, and fine.
Under the rainbow, both hand and hand.
Blessed by God, the woman and the man.

Better Days Are Coming

You are the owner of a used and abused broken
  heart.
Though at the time you thought you would never be
  apart.
Try not to feel sorry, that's sometimes the way
  things go.
You have to be strong now and go along with the
  flow.
Hold your head high, don't take it as a blow.
Pick up the pieces so that your broken heart may be
  sewn.
Take it from me in life, you're really not alone.
Some hearts are made of gold and others of pure
  stone.
I'm telling you this, 'cause you're a sweet-natured
  type of guy.
Things are often not what they seem to be, just
  take it all in stride.
Take time for yourself now and straighten out the
  things you despise.
Relationships of all sorts will come and go bye.
It's all in the mix of your sorrowful puppy eyes.
Don't let the goodness of your heart you possess, go
  astray without thinking things might have
  turned out for the best.
You have many good qualities, my dear Buddy
  Love, Joe.

16

Just open up your heart; when the time is right for
     you,
You'll be the first one to know.

The Intimidator

Did you ever know someone who thought that they
    knew it all?
Until one day Rich met his match and that was
    best of all.
The intelligent and the intellectual are the people
    who succeed.
The bully and the intimidator is someone you only
    call upon in times of distressful need!
The intimidator wants to hurt you with the
    dreadful harsh words that he speaks!
Only the intimidator knows how to get your life in a
    stir,
Never trusting anyone, always making your life
    seem somewhat of a blur.
Open up your eyes right now, never become the
    intimidator's fool.
He thinks about it all the time, playing with your
    mind is his tool.
He doesn't even know that being the intimidator
    just isn't being cool.
All he hears are his very own words, no one can get
    through to him.
He's somewhat like a bull!
He just can't be wrong at anytime, only can he be
    right.
That's why he's called Rich the intimidator,
    because he believes
That he is the king of the night life!

Eye Contact

I moved aside and let you pass.
You turned and said, "Thank you for that."
As I walked away, I turned and glanced.
You were staring at me, as I walked farther past.
You were there, then you were gone, I just couldn't
    see your face anymore.
My eyes touching your eyes was simply no more.
I wish that I could know you, who you are, and
    more.
Your eyes were twinkling, just like the stars.
It's a shame I didn't go back, follow you to get your
    name and know who you are.
Maybe we'll meet again at that very same place,
Where my eyes met your eyes, close up, face to face.

Restless Mind

As I lay myself down to rest, my tired
weary heart along with my tired weary head,
I think to myself, who will be there for me?
All I keep coming up with is me there for you, and
    you there for me!
As I go on thinking, about this, that, and the other,
I close my eyes and go under the covers.
I feel so fortunate that we both have each other.
This is the way when you both love one another.
You loving me and me loving you.
This is what God decided, you for me and me for
    you!

A Best Friend

A best friend is someone who will always be there.
Through thick and thin and in times of despair.
Best friends are forever, also very hard to find.
Don't ever forget this, keep this in your mind.
A best friend will listen and never judge you unfair.
This is one of the good things that we both share.
A best friend like you is the very best of all.
We'll stay friends forever, our friendship stands
     tall.

Water Logged

Sandy beaches, dirty shores.
What's happened to the beautiful coastal shores?
Water turning gray, once was clear-colored blue.
What a shame what the human population can do.
Everything is affected by this way that we have.
Fish and other water species have no control and
      that is what's sad.

Open Hearts

Follow your heart and everything else becomes so
    clear.
Your journey for love is over, you thought you found
    someone dear.
To love and be loved is something that we all crave.
Going together with love come insecurities in so
    many ways.
All the time hoping that opening your heart isn't a
    tragic mistake.
To give love and receive love is the answer to all
    who wait.

Father's Best

To the man I admire and love so.
You taught us everything that you could possibly
     know.
You taught us about life's ins and outs.
You showed us all what fatherhood was all about.
You've worked so hard to give us all the best.
In return, with our love, Dad, we would never give
     you any less.
That's all because you've done a father's very best!

A Mother's Love

A mother is someone whom you'll never doubt.
A mother's love is so special, it's something you just
    can't do without.
A mother is the one who understands her children's
    ways.
A mother's instinct is worth every bit of will it
    takes.
Without a mother's love, there's nothing that can
    replace.
The compassion, the nurturing is just a special
    mother's way.

Money Problems

The root of all time evils, so many foolish mistakes.
Managing a desperate situation without much time
    to contemplate.
Money, more money, never enough to get by.
It's an everyday struggle to just stay alive.
Money for everyone, having no questions asked.
We'd all be so happy, but the economy would fall
    mighty fast.
What are the answers, does anyone know?
People are starving and have no place to go.
Please someone, help these sorrowful souls.

Sunny Day

I rolled up my shirt.
Put out my towel.
Laid it down to be even.
Flat on the ground.
I put on my sunglasses and stared at the clear blue
skies.
All the while the glare of bouncing sunshine looked
right through my eyes.
I lay back and started thinking, then I dozed off to
sleep.
A little while later I heard the sound of something
going beep, beep, beep.
"Are you napping?" asked my friend, then the
telephone rang.
I felt my body tingling!
I knew what I had done.
I had drifted off while lying out in the hot blazing
sun.

Gray-Striped Kitty

Pretty kitty cat, with your gray and white stripes.
So innocent and cute.
All you do is sleep and eat and rub against my shoe.
Playtime so delightful, hanging from your kitty
      tree.
After you've played, you come to cuddle with me.
Purring away, you good friend kitty cat.
This makes me feel that you're perfectly content.
Never any back talk, just a friendly meow.
This is how I know that you're a really great pal.

Judgment Day

The Good Book says never cast out the first falling
stone.
The only one who can judge your life is the man
whom we all know.
God created each of us, individuals of all different
kinds.
People need not judge one another; God will do this
in all good time.
Everyone's born an equal, no better or no worse.
No one can be judgmental while being on this
earth.
Learn how to let go of all the ignorance, along with
all the spite.
Never take on trying to be the judge of someone
else's life.
As the man upstairs looks down upon us,
From the heavens up above, tears are falling from
the skies,
Just your being judgmental doesn't look good
through God's weary, teary eyes.

Wishing on a Dream

Wishes are for dreamers.
Dreamers always wish.
The wishers and the dreamers are people of the
 same type of mix.
The dreamers always take their time.
Dazed out for days, they are one of a kind.
Passing the time in their subtle state of mind.
The wishers on the other hand, wish unrealistically
 at times.
Holding on and grasping to strive to great heights.
Either way you see it, to wait makes no sense.
Make your wishes and dreams a priority in your
 life.
It's all a part of thinking of things in your own best
 interest.

The New Millennium

The age of the new millennium is approaching
indeed.
It's the start of a new millennium, another
thousand years.
Everyone who lives this millennium in time:
consider
yourselves to be the chosen ones, so take it with
great pride.
We are the people of the new millennium.
2000 is the year, many challenges this world will
come to endeavor.
Century after century for the next thousand years.
Lifelong prosperity for the new coming millennium.
Let's help one another and do away with loneliness
and hunger.
In this age of much new discovery, we as the people
are in need of much recovery.
Who really knows what will become or the things in
the world that will be done?
Computers will take over and run, while people will
be having much more fun.
So everyone be glad as you live this new
millennium firsthand.

What Men Like

What do you want?
Are you looking for some hot stuff?
Be slow and take your time, you just
can't get hot stuff off of your mind!
There's really nothing you can do,
just wait, and in time hot stuff will
come looking for you!

The End

In life we meet, reunited at death.
Once we were apart, that just broke my heart.
Soul mates we are, separated for a while.
Brought together our souls, being together our goal.
Bright lights all a flash, pictures of the past.
They are waiting for a while, leaving earth with
    such style.
Scoop us up with the winds towards the light and
    we're in.
This is the end; I say good-bye to family and close
    friends.